Opposites & Visual Skills

Editorial Project Manager
Mara Ellen Guckian

Editor-in-Chief
Sharon Coan, M.S. Ed.

Illustrator
Kelly McMahon

Cover Artist
Brenda DiAntonis

Art Coordinator
Kevin Barnes

Art Director
CJae Froshay

Imaging
Ralph Olmedo, Jr.
Temo Parra

Product Manager
Phil Garcia

Publishers
Rachelle Cracchiolo, M.S. Ed.
Mary Dupuy Smith, M.S. Ed.

Author

Amy DeCastro, M.A.

Teacher Created Materials, Inc.
6421 Industry Way
Westminster, CA 92683
www.teachercreated.com

ISBN-0-7439-3229-3

©2003 Teacher Created Materials, Inc.
Made in U.S.A.

The classroom teacher may reproduce copies of materials in this book for classroom use only. The reproduction of any part for an entire school or school system is strictly prohibited. No part of this publication may be transmitted, stored, or recorded in any form without written permission from the publisher.

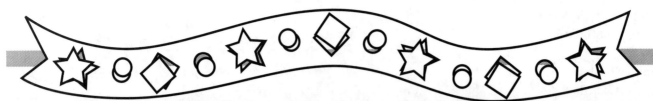

Table of Contents

Introduction 3

Visual Discrimination

Get in Shape 4
Same and Different 5
Fruity Fun 6
Blast Off 7
Can't Catch Me! 8
Cookie Cutter Fun 9
Tea Time 10
Back Together Again 11

Positional Words

Where is the Ball? 12
Clean Up! 13
Triple Scoop 14
Springtime 15
Where's the Bear? 16
Playing at the Park 17
All About Me 18

Opposites

Here or "To Go"? 19
Picking Apples 20
Need a Refill? 21
Hickory, Dickory, Dock 22
Hey Diddle, Diddle 23

Laundry Day 24
Hot and Cold 25
Bubble Bath 26
Sleep Tight 27
Around the Town 28
Matching Opposites 29
Opposites Attract 30
Opposites 31
What's the Opposite? 32
Make the Opposite 33
Game Cards 34–38

Left and Right

Hand and Hand 39
Barnyard Animals 40
Set the Table 41
Buckle My Shoe 42
Parking Lot 43
Waiting Your Turn 44
My Hands 45
Extra! Extra! 46
A Journey 47
Fish Bowls 48

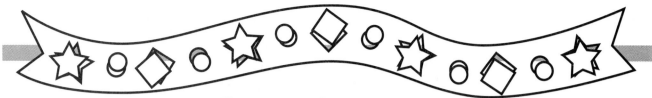

Introduction

Getting children ready for academic success starts early. It is important, in these early years to shape children's attitudes towards school and learning in a positive manner. The ultimate purpose of this wookbook series is to promote children's development and learning in an exciting manner. Young children need lots of repetition. They need directions that are worded in a simple manner. The activities need to be enjoyable and visually stimulating. This series was developed with those goals in mind. Each activity book is designed to introduce young learners to new concepts and to reinforce ones already learned.

Reading plays a vital role in everyone's life on a daily basis. It is, therefore, absolutely necessary that children develop, understand, and learn to apply reading skills at an early age. *Opposites & Visual Skills* teaches students opposites, classifying, understanding the similarities and differences in objects, positional words, and right and left. These are skills children need to enhance language development and to help begin the emergent stages of reading.

You will be delighted as you watch your students discover how interesting and fun learning can be all year long with the gradual sequence of one-page, easy-to-follow, enjoyable practice activities. The pages are great for enrichment, classroom practice, tutoring, home schooling, or just for fun.

Reading skills are the foundation on which every child's education will rest. That is why *Opposites & Visual Skills* is so important. The worksheets in this book can help students build skills that will strengthen comprehension—a major building block of reading and communication. Within this activity book, students will be exposed to four main tasks that will have lasting benefits needed for beginning formal reading.

- **Visual Discrimination:** These pages increase critical thinking skills through classification. Recognizing and comparing likenesses and differences in objects and pictures will help later in the discrimination of numbers and letters.

- **Positional Words:** These pages build and extend knowledge and vocabulary through language concepts and comparison in a concrete, meaningful way.

- **Opposites:** The study of opposites helps stimulate basic thinking skills, use descriptive words, and enhances recall through language development, association, and generalization.

- **Left and Right:** Learning left and right is more than learning an opposite concept. Understanding the concept of left to right will aid children beginning to read. Knowledge of *left* and *right* encourages a natural flow of the proper reading direction and helps develop skills in abstract thinking.

Name _____

Get in Shape

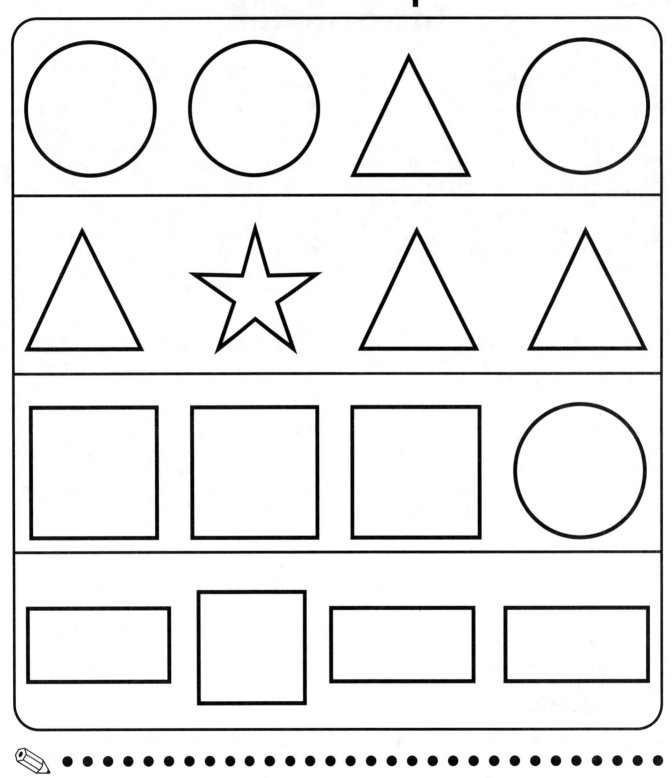

Directions: Look at the shapes. Color the shapes in each row that are the same.

Name _____

Same and Different

Directions: Look at the pictures in each row. Color the pictures in each row that are the same. Cross out the picture that is different.

Name _____

Fruity Fun

Directions: Look closely at the fruit. Cross out the fruit in each row that is different. Color the fruits that are alike.

Name _____

Blast Off

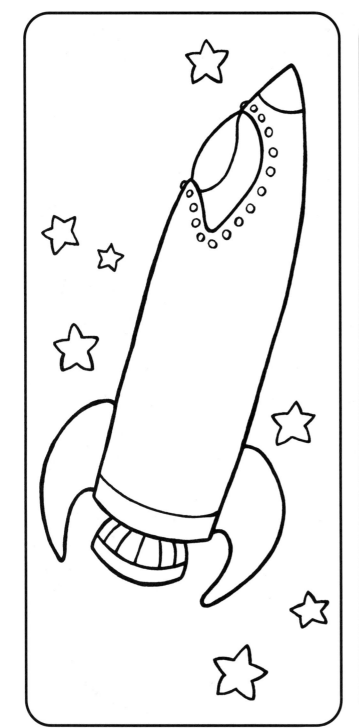
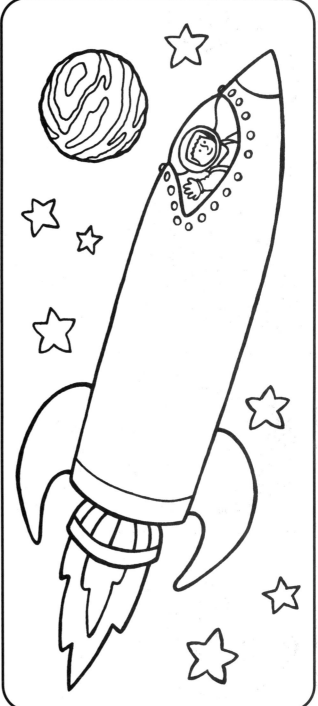

Directions: Look at the two pictures above. Circle three things that are different in the second picture.

Name _____

Can't Catch Me!

 •

Directions: Look at the two gingerbread man cookies. Add the missing parts to the second cookie to make it the same as the first.

#3229 Opposites & Visual Skills   8   © Teacher Created Materials, Inc.

Name _____

Cookie Cutter Fun

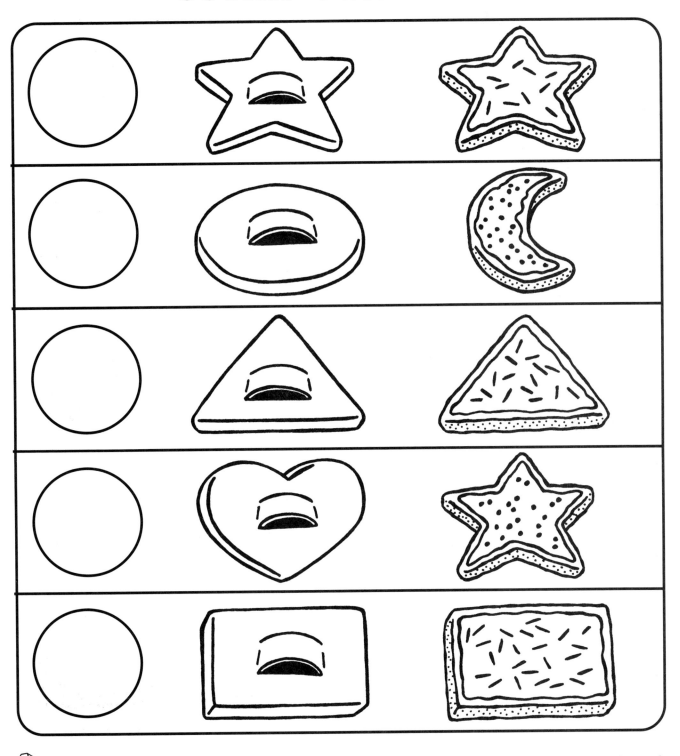

Directions: Draw a happy ☺ face in the circle in front of each row if the cookie shape matches its cookie cutter. Draw a sad ☹ face in the circle if the cookie and the cutter do not have the same shape.

Name _____

Tea Time

Directions: Look at the teapots and cups. Draw a line from the teapot on the left to its matching cup on the right. Color the teapots and the matching cups.

Name _____

Back Together Again

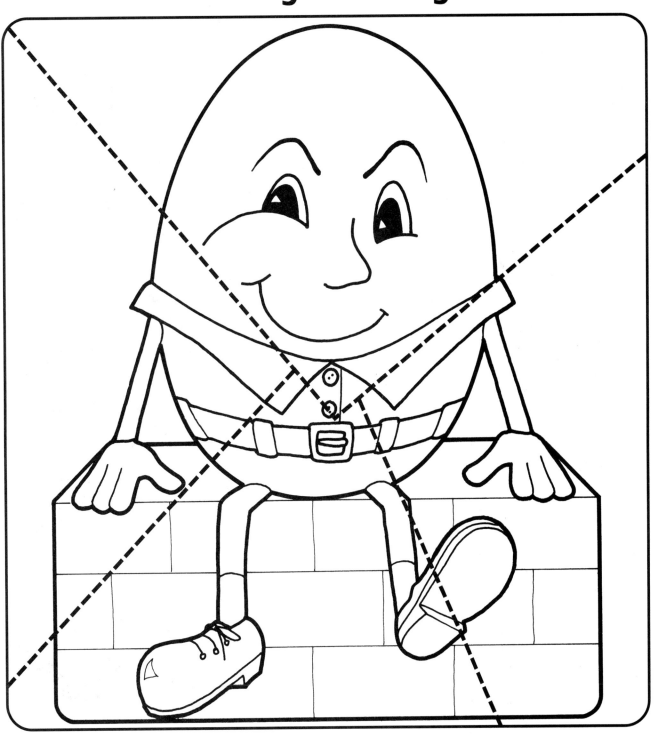

• •

Directions: Color Humpty Dumpty. Have an adult help you cut the puzzle apart on the dotted lines. Put the puzzle back together again.

Optional: Glue the picture onto cardstock before cutting it out.

© Teacher Created Materials, Inc.   11   #3229 Opposites & Visual Skills

Name _____

Where is the Ball?

on

under

beside

between

 •••••••••••••••••••••••••••••••••

Directions: Have an adult read the word in the first column. Look at where the ball is in each picture. Draw a line from the word to the picture that matches that word.

Name _____

Clean Up!

- Glue the teddy bear onto the *middle* shelf.
- Glue the ball onto the *bottom* shelf.
- Glue the toy on the *top* shelf.

 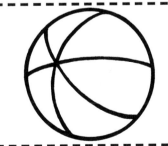 

Directions: The toys are everywhere. Cut out each toy above and follow the directions to help put them away.

© Teacher Created Materials, Inc. 13 #3229 Opposites & Visual Skills

Name _____

Triple Scoop

- Color the *bottom* scoop of ice cream brown.
- Color the *top* scoop of ice cream pink.
- Color the *middle* scoop of ice cream your favorite ice cream color.

 •

Directions: Look at the ice-cream cone. Follow the instructions above to color the ice cream.

#3229 *Opposites & Visual Skills* © Teacher Created Materials, Inc.

Name _____

Springtime

- Draw a sun *above* the bird.
- Draw a flower *between* the trees.
- Draw a worm *under* the ground.

Directions: Follow the directions above to complete the picture. Color the picture.

Name _____

Where's the Bear?

- Put the bear *on* your knee.
- Put the bear *under* your chin.
- Put the bear *between* your knees.
- Put the bear *beside* you.
- Put the bear *behind* your back.
- Put the bear *in front of* your face.
- Move the bear *around* your body.

 •

Directions: Color and cut out the Teddy bear. Glue the Teddy bear to a craft stick. Move the bear, following the directions above.

#3229 Opposites & Visual Skills 16 © Teacher Created Materials, Inc.

Name _____

Playing at the Park

Put the boy *on* the ladder.
Put the ball *under* the slide.
Put the girl *beside* the slide.
Put the dog *between* the flowers.

Directions: Cut out the objects above and follow the directions in the box.

Name _____

All About Me

- Write your name *above* the head.
- Draw a circle *beside* the shirt pocket.
- Write your age *on* the shirt.
- Draw some hair *under* the hat.

 •

Directions: Decorate the person to look like you by following the directions.

Name _____

Here or "To Go"?

Directions: Circle the small item in each bag. Draw a square around the big item in each bag. Color your favorite foods.

Name _____

Picking Apples

Directions: Look at the tree. Color all the large apples on the tree red. Color the small apples on the tree green.

Name _____

Need a Refill?

Directions: Cut out the drink containers above. Glue the ones that are full into the **Full** box and the ones that are empty into the **Empty** box.

Name _____

Hickory, Dickory, Dock

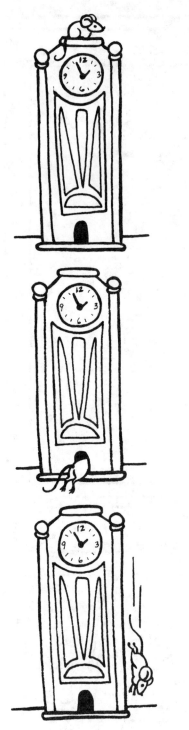

Directions: Look at what the mouse is doing in each picture on the left. Draw a line from each mouse on the left to one doing the opposite on the right.

#3229 Opposites & Visual Skills © Teacher Created Materials, Inc.

Name _____

Hey Diddle, Diddle

Directions: Look at what the character is doing in each picture on the left. Draw a line from each character on the left to one doing the opposite on the right.

© Teacher Created Materials, Inc. 23 #3229 Opposites & Visual Skills

Name _____

Laundry Day

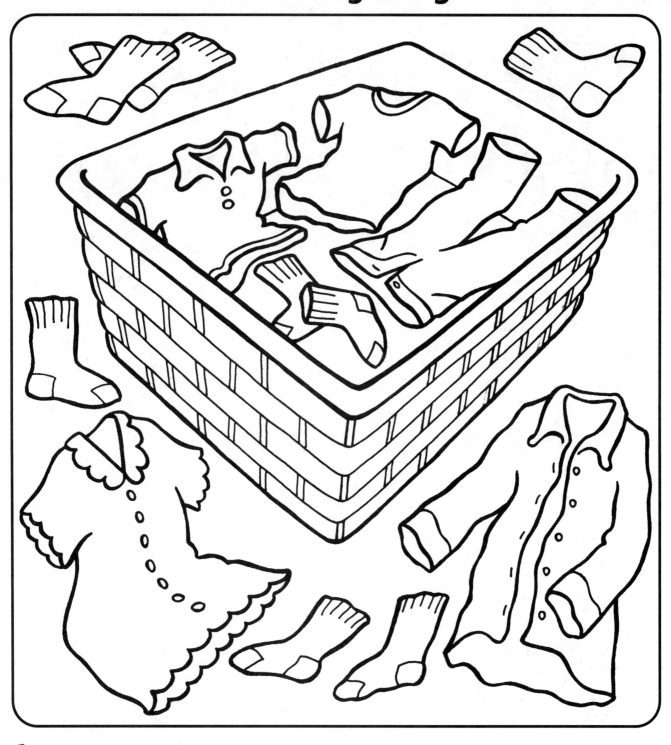

Directions: Color the clothes inside the laundry basket orange. Color the clothes outside the laundry basket green.

Name _____

Hot and Cold

Directions: Look at the items above. Use a red crayon to color the items that could be hot. Use a blue crayon to color the items that could be cold.

Name _____

Bubble Bath

Word Box

above	clean	dry	full
below	dirty	empty	wet

Directions: Look at the first picture in each row. Color one of the two pictures in each row that shows the opposite of the first picture. Use the words in the Word Box as clues.

Name _____

Sleep Tight

Directions: Color the picture in each row that shows the opposite of the picture in the first box.

Name _____

Around the Town

  •

Directions: Cut out the pictures above and paste each one near the picture that shows the opposite.

Name _____

Matching Opposites

Directions: Cut out the pictures above and paste each one next to the picture that shows the opposite. The labels for the pictures are clues!

Name _____

Opposites Attract

 •

Directions: Draw a line from the picture on the left to the matching opposite picture on the right.

Name _____

Opposites

Directions: Draw a line from the picture on the left to the matching opposite on the right.

Name _____

What's the Opposite?

Directions: Draw the opposite next to each picture. Color the pictures.

Name _____

Make the Opposite

girl

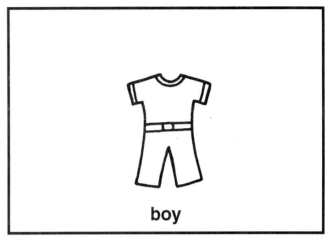
boy

off

on

asleep

awake

 •

Directions: Look at the pictures in the column on the left. Finish drawing the opposite on the picture in the column on the right.

© Teacher Created Materials, Inc.   33   #3229 Opposites & Visual Skills

Name _____

Game Cards

 •

Directions: Color and cut out the opposite cards. Use the cards on pages 34–38 to play matching games, memory games, or the game, Go Fish.

Name _____

Game Cards (cont.)

Directions: Color and cut out the opposite cards. Use the cards on pages 34–38 to play matching games, memory games, or the game, Go Fish.

Name _____

Game Cards (cont.)

Directions: Color and cut out the opposite cards. Use the cards on pages 34–38 to play matching games, memory games, or the game, Go Fish.

Name _____

Game Cards (cont.)

Directions: Color and cut out the opposite cards. Use the cards on pages 34–38 to play matching games, memory games, or the game, Go Fish.

Name _____

Game Cards (cont.)

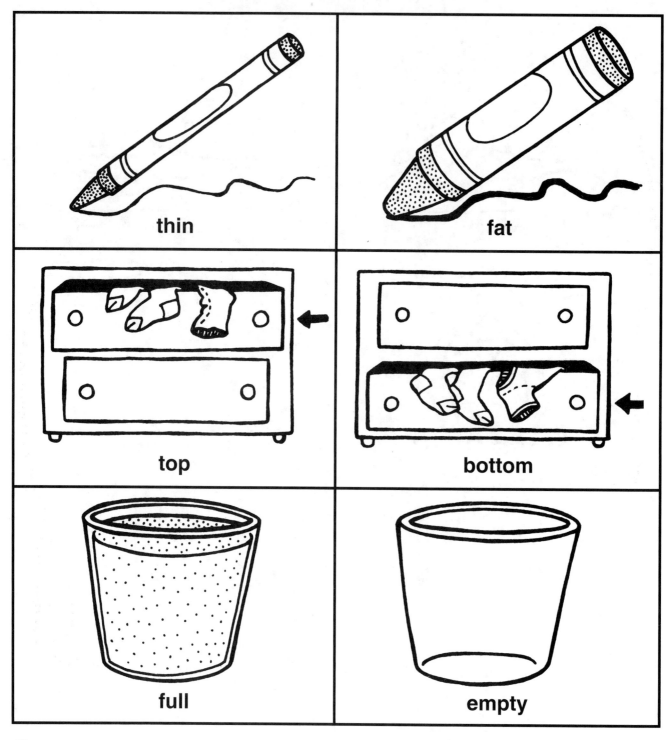

 •

Directions: Color and cut out the opposite cards. Use the cards on pages 34–38 to play matching games, memory games, or the game, Go Fish.

Name _____

Hand and Hand

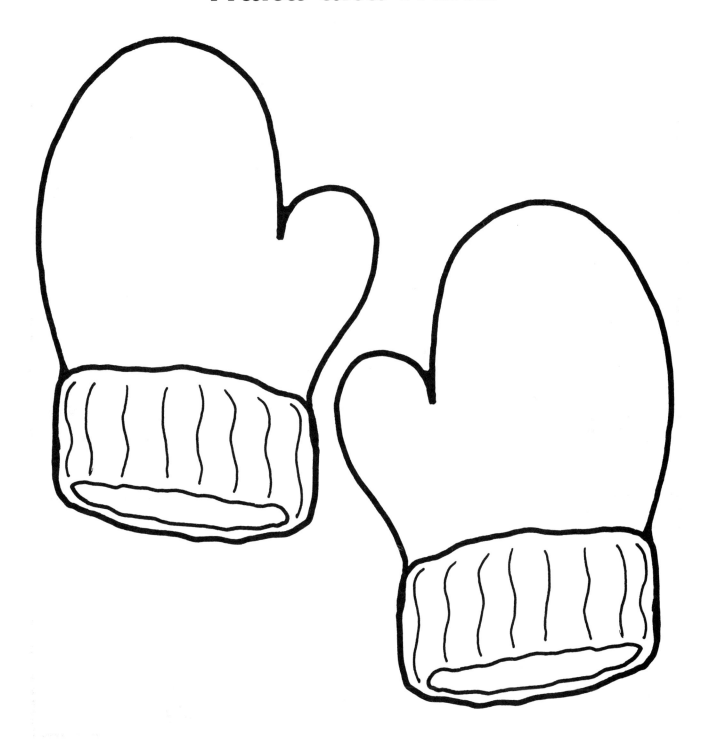

Directions: Put a square under the *left* mitten. Put a triangle above the *right* mitten. Decorate the mitten on the *left* with stripes. Decorate the mitten on the *right* with polka dots.

Name _____

Barnyard Animals

 •

Directions: Color the cow on the *left* side of the barn black. Color the cow on the *right* side of the barn brown. Color the chicken on the *right* yellow and the chicken on the *left* red. Leave the *middle* chicken white.

Name _____

Set the Table

Directions: Draw a spoon and knife on the *right* side of the plate. Draw a fork on the *left* side of the plate. Add your favorite food to the plate.

Name _____

Buckle My Shoe

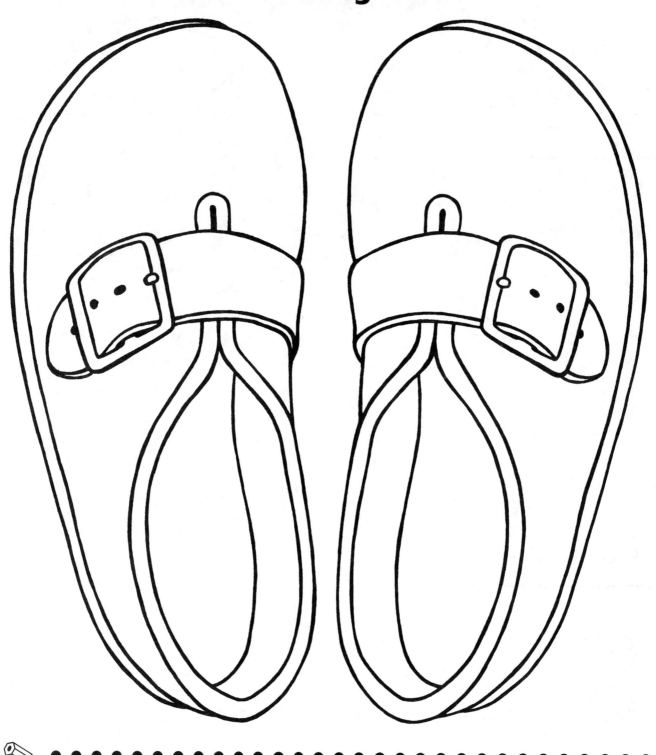

Directions: Decorate the *left* shoe with polka dots. Decorate the *right* shoe with stripes.

#3229 Opposites & Visual Skills   42   © Teacher Created Materials, Inc.

Name _____

Parking Lot

Directions: Color the vehicle in each row that is facing *left*. Cross out the other vehicles.

Name _____

Waiting Your Turn

Directions: Draw a hat on the person in each line who is facing *right*.

Name _____

My Hands

 •

Directions: Trace your *left* hand over the **L**. Trace your *right* hand over the **R**. Color your *left* hand purple. Color your *right* hand green.

Name _____

Extra! Extra!

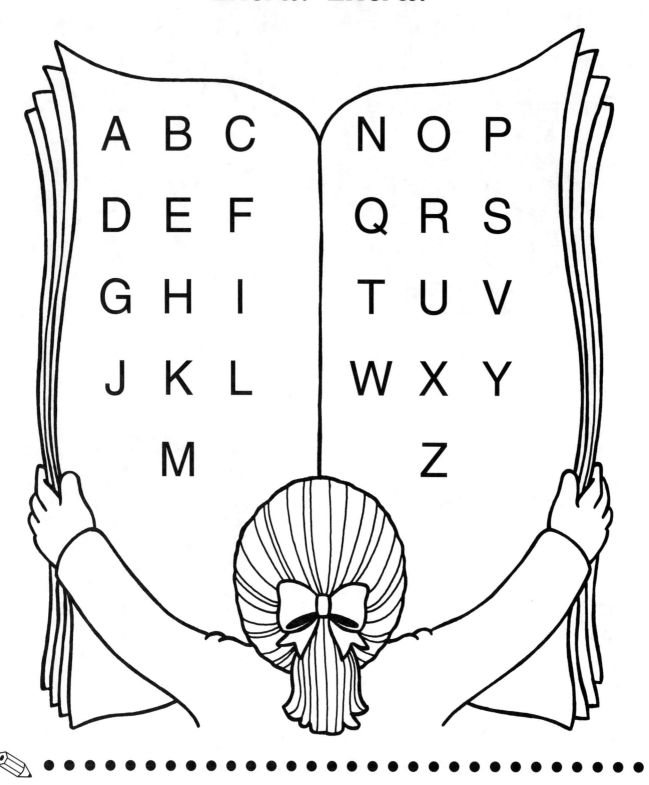

Directions: Underline the letters on the *right* side of the newspaper. Circle the letters on the *left* side of the newspaper.

Name _____

A Journey

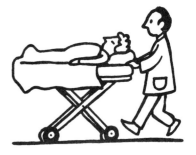

 •

Directions: Draw a line from the vehicles on the *left* to their destinations on the *right*.

Name _____

Fish Bowls

- Draw 3 green fish in the fish bowl on the *left*.
- Draw 4 red fish in the fish bowl on the *right*.

- Draw 2 yellow fish in the fish bowl on the *left*.
- Draw 5 blue fish in the fish bowl on the *right*.

Directions: Look at the two fishbowls in each row. Follow the instructions below each set of fishbowls to add fish to the bowls.

#3229 Opposites & Visual Skills   © Teacher Created Materials, Inc.